SAT
ACT
Mastery

Craig Gehring

ISBN: 061560868X
ISBN-13: 978-0615608686

LR-31914

DEDICATION

To my wonderful wife, Brittany. We fell in love in high school and since then not a day has gone by where you haven't made my life bright.

CONTENTS

 *Get Free ACT Prep by This Book's Author...*

With your purchase of *SAT ACT Mastery*, you have gained access to free ACT prep by this book's author, Craig Gehring, who made perfect scores on the ACT and the SAT. Take advantage of this special offer by visiting the website below:

Visit
www.actmastery.org/free

Chapter 1
The Secret: The End of the Book First

I'm going to level with you.

When I was in high school this is something I would have never admitted.

When I took the ACT during my junior year of high school, I did not blank out once. I ran into a couple questions I had to come back to. I thought I might have gotten one question incorrect.

When I got my perfect score in the mail, I wasn't surprised. I was elated, but it was definitely something I expected.

It was the same with the SAT. When I opened up the envelope with the scores, I was blown away, and could not resist the cliché fist pump, but it was a victory that I knew was coming.

I felt that my education at the time was bigger than the test. It was like I was taking a test a couple grade levels too low. In other words, I was running in varsity track against a freshman team.

You don't want to come off as arrogant or stuck up, especially in high school of all places, so I kept this to myself. A reporter asked me about my prep for the tests, and he was able to find out that I had done very little, but I tried to keep this from getting played up too much.

After the news ran the article and TV feature on my perfect scores, my school got some calls from parents in Baton Rouge. They wanted to talk to me about tutoring their kids. I started giving tutoring sessions on the ACT and SAT and helped a few students pick up their scores. In Louisiana, as in many other states, these scores can make the difference between a fully-paid scholarship to college and nothing at all.

I got some results walking these students through test questions, and made some parents very happy, but I was left with a nagging doubt about how I was helping them. I was doing the same thing that all the ACT and SAT prep classes do – walking the student through the test, mastering each skill one at a time, giving general test taking advice. But the truth was that I didn't get my scores that way. There was definitely a path that I took to master the ACT and SAT, but it looked nothing like modern ACT and SAT test prep.

I tried to write a book on it several times. I never got anywhere with it. I kept trying to write my own version of a Princeton Review or SAT For Dummies.

What I really should have done was try to write this book.

This book will tell you how I got my perfect scores. It will tell you how you can master any test and any subject. You can use it however you'd like, but there's the catch. You've got to use it for it to work.

Now I'm going to level with you on another thing. If you read this book two weeks before you take the ACT, you'll probably score an extra point or two. You might get an extra fifty or hundred points on the SAT. But if you share this with your younger sibling, he or she will do much better than that.

An education is very much like a sport. You can't go from playing flag football to the NFL in two weeks. You've got to build to it. It takes exercise.

This book tells you how to master education. It brings you to the head of the class, and it helps you to stay there.

I'm going to share the secret right now, in the front of the book, and keep sharing it again and again. It will come to you as your own at some point, phrased in your own way.

You have to think of it this way: your P.E. coach asks you to run a mile. You haven't run at all, all year, so you have a lot of trouble with it. You get a C. But the guys on the track team run the mile with a smile on their face. It's easy for them, so easy they just goof off the whole run. Each gets an A+ and is barely sweating at the end of it.

School is the same way. If you're in shape, you can be like the guys on the track team. If you're not, you're always struggling.

Of course, if you're already in shape, it's easier to stay in shape. If you're out of shape, it's harder to get back in shape.

The typical A student finds school to be easy. The typical C student finds school to be difficult. The C student has to put a lot more effort into school than the A student.

The ACT and the SAT are easy if you're in shape.

Tests are easy if you're in shape.

School is easy if you are in shape.

I'll give you another example of this. I used to run cross country, so I use a lot of running examples.

In high school cross country, you get up to the point where you're running five or more miles per day. You get to the point where your parents wish they had stock in Adidas.

In cross country training, there is a concept called "Reserve Miles". Basically, you have to run as many miles as you can at an easy pace, each and every day. This will let you build up a reserve of endurance.

During the summer, I read about this and started running an extra five miles each day. It became very easy running after a while. I wasn't doing anything too strenuous once I got used to it.

When I got back to fall practice, I was way ahead of the rest of the crew. The coach's practice schedules were much easier. The whole year before, I was exhausted and dead after every practice. Now it was easy. I was performing at the same level as the "real athletes" that I was running against the year before.

Then I got sick with bronchitis. I didn't practice for a month and a half. I was back in the rut again and quit soon after. I told everyone I wanted more time with my girlfriend. I had a car now; I had a life. Actually I was just sick of it. After being on top, and realizing how easy it was and how great it was, I couldn't stand struggling through it all again.

The moral of the story isn't to quit things. I'm just being honest with you here. My point is that your ability, in a sport, or in school, is determined by how ahead or behind you are. Only when you get to the very highest ends of the spectrum of training does innate ability or genetics play a dominant role.

For example, until a piano player has mastered all of the general training that goes into playing piano, he or she will always be worse than the player who has mastered all these things – regardless of the factors of natural ability or talent.

Unfortunately, the concept of "smart kid" or "bright kid" and "dumb kid" or "dim kid" is introduced very early to school children. But there isn't any part of elementary school, middle school, or high school that can't be totally mastered by a student, including the SAT. There may be limits to the average human brain, but it certainly doesn't ever reach those limits from anything in high school.

If you work on getting ahead, instead of just working on dealing with the immediate problems, eventually you won't have any big problems to deal with. You won't be struggling. It will be easy.

It's sort of like if you have a hole in your boat, and you keep frantically bucketing out the water, you might survive to the shore. But it was hell. Then again, if you plug up the hole first, and then bucket out the water, you might actually enjoy your boat trip, and get where you're going faster, too!

Hopefully this book will be your first step toward a more enjoyable boat trip AKA education.

CHAPTER 2
MASTERY

Mastery is an important concept to fully grasp. Mastery is the key to education.

To master means to grasp fully, to understand every part of, to be able to do any part of a subject easily and without really even having to think about it.

Most educational problems have to do with problems of mastery. Most problems in life, I might add, have to do with mastery, period.

People who hate math haven't mastered it. Obviously. But let me give you an example of this.

Let's say you're teaching a child to add. If you teach this child to add, and get him to add 5 plus 4, and 2 plus 3, and do this about 100 times, until he felt pretty confident about adding, you could say that you taught him to add. He would still have to think a little each time he needed to add something, though. When he started adding 23 plus 44, he'd have to think a little harder. After adding comes subtracting, multiplying, dividing, algebra, geometry, calculus. With each new subject, this poor student is thinking harder and slower until he can't think at all!

Here's how to teach a child to add. Get him to add 5 plus 4. Get him adding and have him do it hundreds and hundreds of times, until he can add without thinking. Until he enjoys it. Until he's showing off. He's mastered adding. And then, after you go on to the next math subject, return to adding. Especially if he slows down again.

That's mastery. Mastery seems to take a long time. Actually it's the key to going quickly.

Mastery is something that isn't sought after in modern education. Unless you're aware of it and go after it yourself, it will be hit or miss for you to ever achieve it on any part of any subject.

You can pass a test with only 8 out of 10 answers right. But mastery gets you ten out of ten answers right, and you don't even break a sweat.

You have to fully understand what mastery is to be able to achieve it. The reason for this is because you have to work backwards from mastery in order to work out what you need to do to accomplish it. A lot of times, the road won't be paved for you in the classroom. Don't take this as a curse but as a blessing. It makes your journey to the head of the class all the easier, because no one else knows the path either. You figure it out, and you're on easy street.

Someone who has mastered a subject has no trouble with it. They like the subject. They definitely don't hate it. They can help others with it. They're fast. They don't have any doubts or hesitations or reservations about it. People would say that they are a "whiz" so to speak.

The key to mastery is doing more. In the example of the child adding, the key to mastery was doing more adding.

Here's another example. I got a guitar in high school. I tried to play a Red Hot Chili Peppers song. I couldn't do it. It didn't matter how long

I practiced that Red Hot Chili Peppers song. I couldn't make it happen.

Then I started playing just one chord. I played that chord over and over again trying to make it sound like it was supposed to. But I couldn't do that, either.

So then I played one note. I played that over and over again. I thought I had mastered that, without practicing at all, but actually I had the pressure wrong on the chord, and it didn't sound quite right, and my finger was interfering with the other strings.

I played that over and over again. At some point I could play one note and it sounded great. But I still couldn't play it perfectly without thinking about it. So I kept playing it. Then after I mastered that I played two notes. Then a chord. Then I practiced switching chords.

I would go back to one note, then two notes, then chords, then switching chords to refresh. And very soon I had mastered switching chords.

It was a long road to playing the whole Chili Peppers song, but then I found I could play a whole lot of other things, too.

I did this, and was able to at least teach myself this much on guitar, because I understood the concept of mastery. And if it seems like it's impossible to master the step you are on, you've got to look and see what other things you have failed to master earlier. If you haven't mastered playing one note, you'll never master playing a chord, even if you play that every day.

There are many ways to gain mastery of a subject. This book is dedicated in part to ways I've found to master school subjects. But I'm sure for every one I've discovered you can find a dozen more. The important thing is to know what mastery looks like and feels like.

Here's an exercise: Choose the subject (and by subject I mean any-thing – school, sport, art, performing or other) that you're the best at, hands down. Pick some simple aspect of it that you absolutely know how to do, which sets you apart from your peers. Chances are you have mastered that part of the subject. Chances are you enjoy doing that part. Chances are you're good at it.

That same feeling is what you need to have about every subject you're dealing with in school. And if you do, not only will you get A's, not only will you do great on the SAT – but you'll have in your hands the key to a successful life.

Don't mistake talent for mastery. To do so will close the door of op-portunity to you. Someone who is talented at making people laugh, for example, has probably mastered a few comedic qualities. He knows how to say something goofy at just the right time in just the right way. He knows how to do this because he's mastered it. He's mastered it because he's done it over and over again – sometimes creating no laughs, some-times creating tons of laughs, until he can do it in his sleep.

Sure, at a professional level, you can't be the best just through train-ing. And maybe some subjects can't be mastered by some people. But you can be *one of the best* by just mastering a subject as well as you can.

CHAPTER 3
VOCABULARY

The SAT and the ACT are vocabulary tests.

You thought you got out of vocabulary tests in elementary school.

They should have told you that every test that you've ever taken, in every subject you've ever studied, is a vocabulary test. And they're all vocabulary tests from here on out.

They can test other things, too, besides vocabulary. But if you don't understand the vocabulary, you're going to fail the test no matter what.

Some people think that they are dumb when they truly just don't understand what's really being talked about.

Let's draw from the metaphor in the last chapter. Any subject you're studying is like the Chili Peppers song I was trying to play right off the bat. And the vocabulary is the single notes that you have to learn to play first.

There is plenty of literature that scientifically links vocabulary to testing performance on the SAT and ACT. But let's just look at this with common sense. If you only speak English, and then you moved to France and sat in on a class on science, it would not matter how bright you were or naturally talented you were with regards to science. First you would need to understand the words that were being spoken about the subject.

Of course, if you understood nothing of what was being said, you would understand absolutely zero of the subject. But let's say in the class the teacher speaks 90% English but 10% of the science lesson she only speaks in French. Maybe every tenth word she uses is French instead of English, and you don't know what she means, quite.

Well, if you didn't boost your vocabulary to be able to deal with this, you'd end up like the elementary school student who never masters adding. You would have to think. You'd be fuzzy. You'd get slower and slower and the subject would get harder and harder. You could never quite master the subject. Actually it would just get worse and worse and worse.

I noticed very early on in tutoring a few students on the ACT and SAT that the problem wasn't that they didn't have the ability to figure out the problem on the test. They had the mental faculties to be able to do it. But they really didn't understand what was being asked. And this was a problem of vocabulary.

If you're reading something over your vocabulary level, you're going to feel sort of lost, just like you have been thrust in the middle of a French class room. And in a testing environment, like the ACT and SAT, this can be deadly.

The SAT and ACT were easy for me because I understood almost all of the words on the test. Sure you can get by on context clues – but context clues are the same as using your fingers to add. You're going to slow down and you're going to have a lot of problems. Better to understand all of it.

You're not going to do well on the SAT and the ACT unless you have a college-level vocabulary. And that includes the vocabulary of math. That's just the fact. That's the level of mastery required. You don't need an 11th grade vocabulary. You need a college-level vocabulary, and a good one at that.

To take this a step further: you're not going to do well in school unless you have a vocabulary level that is a good bit higher than the grade that you are in.

The wonderful thing about vocabulary is that although it is hugely important, it's also something that can always be learned. It's one of the mind's most basic faculties to be able to memorize what something is. It's one of the first things it does for you in the business of living: it lets you identify who your mommy and daddy are and what it means when they say "Hello" and "Food" and whatnot.

No matter how bad you are in a subject, you can always learn vocabulary.

Now you may think that I'm talking about flash cards right now, or talking about those thirty biology terms you need to memorize for the test on Friday. Actually I'm just talking about your overall comprehension of the English language. And additionally I'm talking about any specialized vocabulary or words that you need to know in order to understand a particular subject.

Of course if you're studying to be a mechanic, you have to know the names of all of the parts of an engine. And if you really wanted to master being a mechanic, you would practice knowing the names of all of the parts until you knew them without thinking. But if you didn't have a general vocabulary, you might find it difficult to learn some of the finer points of being a mechanic, especially from a book or from written material.

Now my mechanic example is pretty thin, because actually you could learn to be a mechanic without reading anything, and be quite good at it, provided you had a master for a teacher. But there are many subjects that you'll only learn by reading a book. And there are many subjects where the tests are only given in writing.

How do you master vocabulary?

Well, there are probably a ton of ways to go about it, and I'm not going to pretend to be an expert on this, but I'll tell you how I did it.

It goes back to this concept of mastery.

The first component to an excellent vocabulary is reading.

To build up your vocabulary, read books that you're already comfortable with. Read books that are fun to read. If you're having to struggle through the book, you're not reading the right book, at least for starters. Go back to the books that you've already read and enjoyed and read them again. Look up the words you don't understand in the dictionary.

And when you hit a word that you don't understand, and that you look up, then make up your own sentences with it until you've mastered it in its totality. Don't be satisfied to have a vocabulary full of words that other people say but you don't. Master the words until you feel comfortable using them. If you were studying French only to listen to it, you wouldn't have very much fun on vacation in France.

Chances are, if you only learn a word so that you can hear it or read it, but not say it, you won't have mastered it sufficiently to remember it. So work out how you would say it in sentences. This is a little slow, I'm sure you're thinking, but what else are you doing in school than learning new vocabulary, and applying it to think through things or understand new thoughts?

You could also just ask a teacher or someone else what the word means. But then practice it until you've got it. And make sure they really know what they're talking about! If you get in the habit of using dictionary.com or a dictionary on your phone or something, you'll find it's easier just to look it up yourself than ask somebody.

If you skip over these words, and never bother to learn what they really mean, then things will get tougher and tougher, and you'll have to think more and more in order to figure things out in school.

It's not quite fun, doing this. That's part of mastery. If you really know what mastery is, you know what I'm talking about. It's fun to have mastered something. It's not quite fun to go through the process of mastering something, though. It's definitely challenging and full of moments of frustration, of dullness, of contentment, and even happiness. But it doesn't get fun until you've really mastered it.

When you see the guy dunking the basketball with a huge smile on his face, you're seeing mastery. You aren't seeing the thousands of lay-ups and dunks that led up to that one. The process can be dull and even frustrating, but the end result is always worth it. And you'll find that once you know that there is mastery up ahead, even the practice becomes dully pleasurable. You start to look forward to the time you can put toward learning something new, and you start to enjoy the little bits of progress leading up to your star-high goal.

I helped put together a free tutoring program for at-risk youth one year. One 2nd grader who was flunking out of his reading class was having trouble in the tutoring sessions. So I got his tutor to just get him to read a simple book out loud, and every time he tripped up, I had her help him understand what the words meant. And then when he got through the book, he read the same one again, and again, and again.

A funny thing happened, something that was completely unexpected. He started getting A's in his reading class.

Obviously we didn't really patch up anything for this student in terms of his reading class, or his next test, or even improve his reading level that much. I can only attribute this wild success story to the fact that the young boy was kept at something until he mastered it, and when he saw how pleasurable it was to master something in school, it became worth it to him to go through the process of school and continue mastering things. In second grade, you only get bad grades if you're unwilling to participate. At least, that's my take and only explanation of what had happened.

To master vocabulary I guess you could use flash cards or memory tricks. You could do any or all of these things. But if you had the intention to master the English language, then every day would provide you with opportunities to improve your vocabulary. Simply listening to what people say and finding out what they mean, and reading what people say and finding out exactly what they mean, could be enough. But you'd have to read enough and listen enough and actually find out the answers to what you didn't understand.

With regards to school, I was fortunate enough to stumble upon this concept of mastery before I entered first grade. (Unfortunately, I didn't ever figure it out with regards to talking to girls.) (Fortunately, my wife had it figured out with regards to talking to boys.)

In the summer before the first grade, my mom punished me. It was one of those awful, unforgivable punishments, you know? I had to stay in my room on my bed for an hour or something. Well, I was going to show her! I was going to take lemons and make lemonade. I grabbed the book that was going to be my school reader for the year, and I started reading. And I stayed on my bed for hours and hours, long after my punishment was over.

I had a dull awareness then of something – that something good was happening. The next day I kept reading. It didn't take long for me to read the entire reader, cover to cover. Did I understand every word of it? Absolutely not.

But when I went to class, I was absolutely at the head. Not really because I had any special qualities over my peers. It was that I had cheated. And when I say cheated, I mean that in the most literal sense. I had the most unfair of advantages. I'd already read the book!

I was in shape, so to speak. I'd spent a little bit of my time in the summer getting fit. And now everything thrown at me in that class was a breeze. I was able to draw a lot more meaning out of what the teacher said. And since I knew a lot of this, the teacher even gave me work from the next year's reader. MORE CHEATING!

I got As because I was ahead of the curve. I was minimally at a second grade reading level in first grade.

Look at it this way. If I had started just one year ahead of everyone else, and then just studied enough to move forward one grade level every year, I would be at the head of the class every year. Do you see how that works? I would have to do the same amount of work as everyone else. But because I started a year ahead, I get the A.

The other way to look at it is this: imagine the student who starts a year behind. For whatever reason by the time he hits fifth grade he is only at a fourth grade reading level. Well he'll be at the bottom of the class every year, even if he works just as hard or harder than the kid at the top of the class. And since he's behind, it gets harder and harder to understand the lessons, so he falls even more behind.

So there is definitely a natural born or genetically endowed intelligence. Science has discovered that. But you can't discount the fact that if you took two people born with identical intelligences, and you put one a year behind and one a year ahead, that the one who is a year ahead would have a much easier time and get better grades. The one behind would have a harder time and get worse grades. *Even if they worked just as hard as one another and both had exactly the same mental gifts.*

My point here is to cheat. In other words, get an unfair advantage. Don't do the thing all your peers are doing, which is simply going through classes and downloading the information from the teacher. Do instead what it will take to master your subject. And win.

In the summer before I took the ACT and SAT, I picked up a sci-fi book I had put down a dozen times. A very literate friend of mine had recommended it to me, but the vocabulary was upper college level. I love a good sci-fi book, but the words made it a little slow going. I decided to just sit down with a dictionary at my side and get through that book.

At first it was frustrating, but then I picked up a rhythm. It started to feel like that day in elementary school where I learned how to dribble a basketball. I started to enjoy it.

After that, I had grown brazen. I was looking for a fight. So I picked up a Shakespeare play that I'd always wanted to read but never could get through. I loved theatre but could never really understand Shake-speare. And with two dictionaries at hand, including one special for Shakespearean words, I got through it. But then I couldn't get enough. In that summer I think I read ten of Shakespeare's plays, mastering the words as I went.

I kept reading. And by August, my vocabulary was beyond what the SAT was testing.

There was a lot of groundwork to get there, though. There's a lot of vocabulary to build up to that. But the point is that 90% of the problems you may have with the SAT will go away if you have a college-level vocabulary. And that just takes reading and insisting on learning the meanings of the words.

Chapter 4
The Secret of Math

There is a secret to math. If you don't recognize it, you'll always have a hard time with it.

Math is a shortcut. You're training your brain to do something that it does not naturally do all by itself. You're training it to know that when you have two apples and two apples you have four apples. And then you're training it from there to know that two of something plus two of something is four of something. And then we go one step more. We learn that two plus two is four!

"Two of what?" you ask.

"Well, just two!" says teacher. And either that makes sense to you in that moment, or you hate math.

Math can be likened to ninja training. A ninja practices blocking a punch over and over again. Eventually he learns what it looks like when someone is about to hit him. In his brain, that look equals someone hitting him. So he reacts to the look instead of reacting to the point where he's actually getting hit. And so he has faster reflexes. Actually he trained in a shortcut in his brain.

Math is the same way. Once you learn without a shadow of a doubt that two of something plus two of something is four of something, you don't have to actually count out the apples anymore. And eventually you know that rule holds true for anything, including tacos, stars and space shuttles. Eventually you train it into your brain that four plus seven is eleven, and you know it so well that you don't add it any more, the number eleven just appears in your mind.

If you forget that math is a shortcut, you'll have a problem when you enter into the dreaded realm of the word problem (which means you'll have a problem on the ACT and SAT as well). That's because you won't know what math tool to apply because you won't know what the shortcuts are for.

Like ninja training, if you don't have your basic math training down, you won't go very far. If you are studying algebra for the ACT, but are still counting out your times tables in your head or have to use a calculator – forget about it. Spend your time mastering your times tables and only come back to the more advanced math material once you're comfortable. You'll be amazed at how much better you are.

Solving a math problem is like a juggling act. Anybody's brain can only juggle so many balls at a time. And if two thirds of your attention is devoted to figuring out what seven times six is equal to, you may as well just go home. Anything that you can do to clarify the problem, and reduce the strain on your mind to solving it, will bring you one step closer to your goal of a correct answer.

I haven't tutored a ton of students, but every student that I have tutored in math that was having trouble showed signs of a lack of mastery in their basic math skills. Here I was helping them understand geometry, and they couldn't figure out the angle of the triangle because they divided the numbers incorrectly.

Let me say this again: even if the student can with some effort get these basic operations of addition, subtraction, multiplication, and division correct, it takes an effortless mastery to really get far in math. There is a lot more practice involved in math than in any other academic subject. That's because you're training your brain.

You're not just memorizing facts. You're teaching your brain how to think – and how to think correctly and quickly.

Math came about because people found that numbers behave in certain ways. When you know the rules about how numbers behave, you can do things quicker in your mind. And you can figure things out that no one could ever figure out without the rules there.

All the different types of math are just shortcuts for different categories of problems.

ARITHMETIC teaches you the rules about adding, subtracting, multiplying and dividing things so that you can quickly figure out how much of something there is. Arithmetic lets you quickly figure out whether you're better off paying for your car in cash or in 36 easy payments of $999.99.

ALGEBRA gives you shortcuts to solving problems. It helps you figure out what one or more unknown quantities are. Algebra could help you figure out, for example, how many hours you need to work each week to keep up with your bills.

GEOMETRY teaches shortcuts in figuring out the sizes and properties of shapes. For example, mathematicians discovered ways to calculate the angles and lengths of a triangle without having to measure them with a ruler. Navigators used to use geometry to figure out where on the oceans they were (and satellites use much more complicated geometry to tell you the same on your iPhone.)

TRIGONOMETRY gives you even more complex shortcuts about triangles, building on what you have already learned in geometry.

CALCULUS gives you shortcuts to figure out things that change over time. This lets you figure out complicated things, like the area of a curvy shape, or how much rocket fuel you'd need to blast a ship into outer space.

Math builds from one subject to the next. But you can't ever forget that they are shortcuts. They have to be practiced. A lot of math doesn't naturally "make sense". If it did, you wouldn't have to study it. But when you practice it over and over again, you start to be able to make sense of it. And if you continue to solve math problems in the subject, you begin to master it.

What does mastery consist of?

Until you can take a sheet full of multiplication problems, and fill them out in about the same amount of time it takes just to write the answers, you should probably still work on memorizing your multiplication.

There are plenty of subjects where there's no reason to memorize random facts. But math is not one of them.

You've got to do the same type of problems over and over again until you can solve them by yourself without reference to the book. Until they're hardwired into your brain.

View math the same as learning to play the piano and you're barking up the right tree. Except everyone is required to do it or they flunk out of school.

I strongly recommend that you cheat. In other words, read the book. Very rarely do teachers get you to work step by step through the book. Do the whole book in the summer. Relax and have fun through the school year. You think that sounds crazy but you'll be surprised how little time it takes to work through a good bit of the book.

The problems are key. You have to solve the problems and keep working them over until you master them.

A note for tutors: if your student gets a math problem wrong, keep working him through similar problems until he starts getting them right. And then keep working him through similar problems that you make up until there's a big smile on his face and he's confident and doing it easily. And then go on to something else and then swing right back to that same group of problems and do more. If he had a problem with a math area on Monday, ask him similar questions on Friday, and the next month, and the next, until you're confident he's mastered it.

It takes a lot longer to master a skill than it does to be "pretty good" at it. You might have to solve 20 problems to be good at it but 100 to really master it.

Math is the most unforgiving of subjects when it comes to the necessity of mastery. Each component of math builds on the previous component. Without addition, subtraction is difficult. Without subtraction, division is impossible. Without all of arithmetic, you'll be in the woods on algebra. And don't try geometry without a firm grasp of algebra. And so it goes. If you don't have a firm grasp of each part, you'll have trouble with the rest.

CRAIG GEHRING

CHAPTER 5
MEMORY TRICKS

One step to mastery is memorization. I talked about memorization a lot in the last chapter on math. If you can't remember all of the important parts of a subject without even thinking about them, you are going to have trouble with that subject.

It's all very well for me to tell you that you have to memorize things, but if I don't help you do it, the advice is pretty worthless.

I'm going to give you a couple ways that I memorize things that are very easy. Actually I'm going to give you the key to memorization, and then you'll be able to come up with ways to memorize things that work for you.

Have you ever met someone at a party, and he told you his name, but in the next second, you forgot it? You definitely heard it, but it was like it slid off your mind back into the air in an instant. You end up having to ask your friend who that guy is, and usually your friend doesn't remember either.

The reason for this is that your mind didn't feel that this guy's name was very important. It didn't feel like it needed to go to the effort of recalling that name.

That's not the trick, though. If that were it, all you'd have to do is psych yourself out while you're reading your biology book. "If I don't memorize the different stages of a cell splitting, the world will come to an end!" Unfortunately, that doesn't work.

As a matter of fact, probably you've had the experience of forgetting the name, and so you said to yourself, "Well, that was very rude of me. I'm going to have to focus here. I'm going to have to try really hard to remember names. The next person that I see, I'm going to remember their name, so help me!"

When you shake hands with the next guy, you say to yourself, "His name is Joe! That's important! I'm going to remember that one!" Maybe you remember the name throughout the party. But the next day when you try to say something about him, you have to refer to him as, "that guy," or "John's friend."

The reason for this is that your brain doesn't remember things like facts based on how alarming they are. It's too smart for that. It doesn't remember things based on how badly you want to remember them. It remembers things based on how truly important they are.

Based on my experience with memorization, and in trying to learn subjects, and teach other people subjects, I think the brain figures out how important something is based on how many other pieces of information it's related to, and how important those other things are.

I am not a neurosurgeon, and in all likelihood this isn't even vaguely what really happens in the brain when you're trying to remember something, but it's a good illustration and can help you understand how best to memorize things.

Imagine the brain for a moment. It is a mass of neurons. These neurons are all connected, and send electricity back and forth from one to another in an effort to calculate and think. There are an uncountable number of neurons in the brain. Suppose memories are stored in the neurons. The more a memory affects your understanding of other memories, the more relevant it is to your experience (i.e. the more important it is) the more neurons it affects. In other words, you could say that some memories are bigger than others. Some memories affect more brain area than others.

Now when you try to remember something, your brain is calling up or reactivating some of those neurons. And if it can hit on some of those neurons, the whole memory comes up. But if it's a small memory, you might have to hunt around for a while. Have you ever had the experience of having to "rack your brain" for a memory? Well in this illustration, that would be your brain firing impulses into the dark until it found a neuron that had been touched before by that memory.

The secret to remembering something is to make the memory as big as possible. This isn't done by just thinking big thoughts. It's done by lacing the memory with other memories, by relating this piece of information with other pieces of information, over and over again until it's a part of the whole.

When a memory is part of your overall experience, and laced with your understanding of many other things, it's extremely easy to call it up.

Someone who is good at memorizing and learning could be said to be good at weaving. Only, instead of weaving thread or fabric, you're weaving information in your mind.

I'm sure you heard of the memory trick of associating something funny with a word in order to be able to remember its definition. My friend once remembered the definition of the word "ebullient" (meaning cheerful and full of energy) by imagining the most cheerful girl he knew riding a bull. By relating the word to a funny image and a person who he was close to, he was able to recall the definition of ebullient.

The reason why this worked was because he related something new to something that he already understood. The more interconnected he makes the new piece of information to the information he already understands, the firmer it's going to be in his mind.

You don't have to use memory tricks to make this work. In learning a new word, it would be best to go over the definition of the word in your mind several times. Then make up sentences of your own choosing using the word. You could also read other peoples' sentences using the word. If you tried to remember other times you had heard the word, but didn't remember what it meant, that would help. And then if you thought of what other words you know that are similar to this new word, that would help more. You could even take it one step further: how is this word different from the words I already know? How is it the same as some of these words?

In the same amount of time, learning the word this way, you'll have a much better grasp of it than if you just repeated the definition over and over again.

This isn't memorization by repetition. This is memorization by weaving. It's actually natural learning.

It's as though you are weaving a spider web to catch the information in your mind. The more connections you draw to that piece of information, the better off you'll be, the more easily accessible the information will be, and the more you'll learn.

Having trouble remembering an important person in history? Well, start weaving. What other people in that time period are you familiar with? How is this person similar? How is he any different? What was he doing and how did that fit in to what everyone else was doing? How does this person compare to the other people that you're familiar with in the present day? Did his actions have any effect on the course of history? What changes did he make? What did he fail to change?

You start to connect where this person fits in to everyone else, and it gets easier to remember. Sure, you might need to still repeat his name over and over, or test yourself by flashing his picture and remembering who he is, but you'll find something interesting. After you "weave," so to speak, you'll notice that this person seems a lot more substantial in your mind, a lot more memorable. If you forget his name for a second, when you do remember it, a whole treasure trove of info will start coming back, not just a blank.

And then when you add more related information into the spider web, it starts to cement. You start to know it cold. What's fascinating is that the more related information you add to the web, the better and more firmly you understand and can remember the core information.

This is one of the fundamental tenets of my philosophy of study. In order to understand the core of a subject very well, you have to understand a whole lot of related information relatively well. You'll understand a certain historical figure much better if you lightly read up on all the people around him who were influential during that time period, too, and how they related to him. If you spent the same amount of time just cramming your brain only with information about this historical figure, you still won't remember him as well.

I heard that one historian recommended just reading the biographies of the American presidents, in order to gain a firm grasp of American history. This makes sense, actually. By reading about the same periods of time from multiple viewpoints, you'd have a very clear idea of American history by the end of the study. What's more, it would be impossible for you to not remember and be well-informed about the core events of American history. You'd probably have close to a postgraduate understanding of the subject if you did this thoroughly enough.

If the test is on polar bears, please don't just study the twenty facts that are guaranteed to be on the test. You might be able to remember them for the test, but you won't have learned anything. And you probably won't even remember them all for the test. Read about the polar bears. Look over the important facts. Then ask yourself, "Now why are these polar bears important? What do they have to do with what I've already learned." And depending on what is on your mind at the time, a thought might come to you. "Well, I've been reading about ecologies in science. I wonder how these polar bears fit into the ecology." And you look it up and you see they're at the top of the food chain. But you see the first fact that you need to memorize. It says they're nearly extinct. And you ask yourself, "Why are they extinct, if they're at the top of the food chain?" And you Google and find out they were hunted or some such thing or the local medicine men liked their pelts for rituals, etc. Which relates to fact number five which you're going to learn.

Bullet points can never beat a body of knowledge. Bullet points are not the way a human being learns. People develop bodies of knowledge through curiosity, through study, through asking questions. You can't learn from bullet points and expect to have an easy time of it.

You have to give yourself enough time to learn a subject. And you'll be amazed how much time you save when you approach a subject the way I'm discussing it as opposed to just shoving the bullet points on a flashcard flashing them until achieving a hypnotic state of test preparedness.

Memory is best filled actively. If you are actively finding facts, if you are actually SEARCHING in your researching, you'll find that you remember the whole thing a lot better. The brain seems to place more importance on what you do and on what you want to know than on what someone else throws at you.

Is it easier for you to remember a bit of a teacher's lecture, or his answer to the one question that you asked? It's the same with a book. If you're looking, searching, actively learning, then you're naturally going to be interconnecting facts in your mind. The reason for this is because when you are actively learning something, trying to really learn it and understand it, you have to make it fit with what you already know.

Your mind is not a tape recorder. It's a survival mechanism. It's a highly developed machine, and it's there for the primary purpose of keeping you alive and well. Sure, you can use it as a handy tape recorder, too, but why turn study and learning into just memorizing facts when you can instead just learn?

Learning is an active process. No one is going to draw the connections to the new facts you are learning except you. It's impossible for anyone else to do it for you, because it's your mind and your web.

It's been said that some people are visual learners, some are audio learners. Actually anyone could benefit from learning something multiple ways. These create more connections. It's a great idea (at least in my opinion) to watch the movie based on the book after you read the book for English class. As a matter of fact, if you really want to know the book well, watch all three of the movies that have been produced based on the book. And read a couple peoples' commentaries as well.

Clif Notes, despite popular opinion amongst teachers, is not a criminal organization solely responsible for the destruction of the minds of youth and the corruption of the testing system. After you read your assignment, you would do well to read through the Clif Notes and get someone else's take and summary of the material. So long as you don't use the notes to replace the actual material, and you balance what they say with what you already have learned, and you read other material as well, you're going to come away with a much better understanding of the book than if you just read it once or twice and then try to memorize flash cards about it.

Getting a fact from multiple sources and viewpoints is a key to an excellent education. You can't learn something with one pass through. This is contrary to educational thought, which tends to make you study one American History book throughout the year. But if you were to read a few American History books with slightly different focuses, you'd have it down a lot better, and with a lot lighter study.

The mind rejects facts that don't make sense. Without context for facts, they don't make sense, and your brain will tend to reject them. This will make the process of memorizing much more difficult. Try to get as much context for the facts you are learning as possible, and memorization will be much easier.

CHAPTER 6
STANDARDS

Standards are deceptive.

When a teacher sets a standard that he or she expects you to meet, you are walking headlong into a trap without knowing it.

The reason for this is that it is nearly impossible to exactly maintain a certain standard.

For example, if your job were to keep a lobby clean, and the standard was that there could be no more than ten pieces of trash on the floor at a time, you could have quite a hard time maintaining that standard. Why is this?

Well if you tried to keep only ten pieces of trash on the floor, and whenever it got to eleven, you went and scooped two up, you'd be quite worried all the time. You'd be constantly running around, watching people suspiciously who walked out of the elevator, taking out the trash.

The trick is that the way to maintain the standard is to exceed it greatly.

If you were to keep the floor completely clean, and every piece of trash cleaned up, you'd have no problem maintaining the standard set forward. What's more, because the lobby is completely clean, people are less likely to throw trash on the floor. So the answer to a standard is to work out how to greatly exceed the standard, and do that.

In school the teacher develops a standard. It's based on what's in the curriculum. She sits at her desk and creates her lesson plan based on "What does this kid need to know to meet the requirements set forth by the school board?" "What does this kid need to know to be prepared for college?" And she works out the minimum, and that goes into her lecture for the day, and that goes into her test.

We learned in the past chapter that it's nigh impossible to learn isolated facts and make them stick in your mind. You have to learn more to retain a minimum. So in this instance the teacher creates the standard and gives it to you. And if you just do her assignment and listen to her lecture, you're going to barely make that standard. Or you're not. And that's why there are very few classes on Earth where everyone makes As.

Really the way to do well in a subject in school is to actively learn the subject. Your teacher's lessons are part of that. But so is your own study. It doesn't have to be anything arduous. Just read. Just be interested. Ask questions.

I am of the opinion that schools should get their students to read at least five times as much as they make them do. Not all of it needs to be terribly dry or textbook stuff. But if the teacher makes his student overshoot, the student will definitely meet the minimum standard.

There's a saying, "Shoot for the moon and you miss, you'll end up somewhere in the stars." I don't think that's true. First off, you would end up in the Earth's orbit and eventually wind up incinerated in its atmosphere. You definitely wouldn't be in the stars. But I think this is true: "Aim to land on a square inch on the moon, and you'll end up at most a foot away. Aim to land on a square foot, and you'll end up a yard away. Aim to just land anywhere at all on the moon, and don't be surprised if you miss completely." And end up orbiting Earth and incinerating etc. etc.

When you accept someone's standards as your own, you are making it almost impossible for yourself to meet those standards. Set your standards much higher than what is expected, and you'll always meet or exceed expectations.

I have an advertising agency. When I first got into the business, I would do exactly what the customers wanted. I would aim to meet their expectations. When I would do so, they were somewhat satisfied. Sometimes I would fail to do so.

Then I remembered this fact that I had learned from my experiences in school. If they gave me one standard, I set my standard much higher. By following this philosophy, I ended up with happier customers, referrals, and a more prosperous company. You can't please everybody, but you can always do better.

If you're studying the civil war, don't just read the textbook. Watch some History Channel movies. Indulge in a little Wikipedia hunt, learning random facts about that time period. Read not only the assignment from the textbook but the rest as well. And pick up some more reading in the area.

I had a Louisiana history class that I could have slept through because the summer before I read part of a very thorough biography on Lewis and Clark, the famous explorers of the Louisiana Purchase territory.

The fascinating thing about it is that everything that I needed to know for the tests in that class WAS NOT present in the biography I had read. But because I already had so much information about that period of time and geographic area and what was happening, what was said in class and what I had to read stuck in mind very easily. There was already a web to catch it!

By exceeding expectations, on accident as in the above example, or on purpose, you set yourself up to win. The best way to win in education is to cheat. Ignore whatever bar is set for you by your school and instead reach for the stars.

If you only do what's expected of you, you'll earn an average SAT score. And you'll have a mediocre school experience. And that's if you are a model student. That's if you do everything the teacher says. And it will be somewhat difficult and all that.

It's better to "cheat" and just get ahead of the curve.

You've seen the student that was held back a grade in school. Very often he flies through the class the second time through. It's because he's ahead. Often his behavior is better. He has an easier time of it. It's because he's already done the grade! Now that seems painfully obvious, but let's apply that simple truth to the grade that you are in.

Take some steps to get ahead of the curve. You don't have to redo the grade to accomplish that. You just have to do more and be intelligent in choosing what it is you study and learn so that it actually applies to what you are learning.

CHAPTER 7
THE LEARNING WEB

I originally outlined this chapter as "The Learning Tree". I've heard of the concept before as the "Learning Pyramid". But I think a web is actually the best way to explain it.

I'm sure you've heard of the concept before that everything you learn builds on what you've already learned. You have to learn the fundamentals, the most basic parts of a subject, before you can learn the more complicated parts of a subject.

Your learning builds up like a pyramid, with more and more facts built from the base. If you have a faulty base, (such as having trouble with basic multiplication in math) you'll never get far in the subject.

I used to refer to this concept as the "Learning Tree". I chose a tree instead of a pyramid because a graph of your knowledge would look more like a tree. It has a trunk that is your basic knowledge, composed of what you know of the English language and the basic facts of life. It has branches, like mathematics and history. These branches shoot from the trunk. As the trunk grows, so do that branches. At the tips of some of the branches are beautiful flowers – crowning achievements – the points where you have mastered the subject as far as it will go.

You'll never reach the full development of a branch all of a sudden.

You have to grow your education.

I think the best way to look at this, however, is as a spider web. Each subject is its own interconnected web. The more information you add on, the larger your web becomes, and the more firm the basic, fundamental knowledge.

There are some things you can't learn without understanding more basic concepts.

There are some specialized things that you can learn, but only have a flimsy understanding of. Just like a spider could tie a few strands off by themselves; but if they're not connected to the overall whole, they are flimsy indeed.

An education is a matter of quantity, really, not quality. Quality comes about because of a quantity of learning. If you learn enough, then you know a certain amount well.

A spider's web is most perfect at the center, and gets more frayed at the edges. The bigger the web, the bigger the more perfect center.

In your education, you want to learn as much as possible, and try always to relate it to what you already know. In this way you'll build a stronger web.

If you're having trouble, recognize that maybe you're trying to learn something in a subject that you're missing the fundamentals of. Go back and master the fundamentals, then try again. In other words, you may be building a part of your educational web too far from where you've started. You may need to lay down the interconnecting web-work first.

Part of what helps you to spin the learning web are your own questions. Asking why something is the way it is, how it fits into the big picture, will help you to succeed in improving your web.

In order to master something, you have to recognize that your difficulties with learning it may lie not in the subject you're studying but in something earlier. You have to actively seek to repair any part of your education that you are missing.

CRAIG GEHRING

CHAPTER 8
TALENT VS. MASTERY

Talent or intelligence plays a role in education, no question.

Talent can help someone master a subject more quickly.

Talent can separate one master from another.

If a car could have talent, talent would determine how fast the car could accelerate and how high its top speed was.

But the SAT and ACT do not measure talent or intelligence. They measure knowledge and education.

If the SAT were a race, you could say that it measures whether or not you are going at least 80 miles per hour down the road.

It doesn't matter how long it took you to get up to 80 miles per hour. And it doesn't matter how much faster than 80 miles per hour you can go.

So, you see, if you are talented, you could get up to 80 miles per hour faster. If you were particularly intelligent, you could gradually go much faster than 80 miles per hour.

But just about any car can get up to 80 miles per hour.

Any person can meet the standards set forward on the SAT and ACT, if they set their standards much higher and meet them through hard work, active study, and the application of the principles contained in this book.

A lot of debate goes on in this country about whether or not children are receiving a quality education. They talk about whether teachers are qualified and how qualified they are. They talk about whether students are meeting benchmarks and passing standardized tests. Quality is a major part of this debate.

I think quality is important, but nowhere near as important as quantity. We need more education. We need more learning. If we are to meet a specific standard for a multiple choice test, we need to learn five times that much.

In an ideal learning environment, you are restudying for tests very little, and you are actively studying many new things all the time. And these things relate all one to the other so that it constitutes a review of what you've previously covered without you really even having to think about it.

But back to this subject of talent versus mastery: in fields of study that do not tax the upper limits of human ability and intelligence, talent or genetics is not a factor to consider when you're trying to figure out whether someone can succeed or fail.

So let's throw it out.

The ACT and SAT are questions of mastery, not talent or intelligence. If you're a gifted learner, you're in luck. But if you're not a gifted learner, you're in luck as well. Because what you've heard isn't true. You're not a C student. You're behind. And you have all the innate ability and intelligence that you need to get ahead.

CHAPTER 9
THE HIDDEN QUESTIONS

In solving a math word problem, it helps to consider that there are hidden questions.

Before actually starting to solve a math problem, you need to develop the habit of asking a few more questions first.

These questions are:

1) What are they trying to get me to find out?

2) What is it that keeps me from finding the answer?

3) What math tool (shortcut) do I already know that will give me the answer?

These questions are very powerful.

Try asking these questions the next time you're helping someone solve a math problem. Once they answer your questions, they may very well find that they can answer the question on the test, too!

Usually the answer to the first question, "What are they trying to get me to find out?" is basically the same as the last sentence in the word problem. It doesn't take a lot of detective work but it serves to fix in your mind the destination of all your work. You're posting a "I'm supposed to end up here!" in your mind.

One of the problems of working out a math problem is that you're dealing with shortcuts for counting things up that don't actually exist in the real world. Instead of counting real apples, you're counting apples in your head. And only so many apples can fit in your head!

Everybody has hit a disorienting point in a math problem before where they have a, "Wait, what was I doing?" moment. Question 1 helps you to stay focused and avoid getting lost as much as possible.

The second question, "What is it that keeps me from finding the answer?" helps you to identify the barrier. In other words, "What did the test do to hide the answer from me?" You'll end up with an answer to this question like, "Well, this would be obvious except they told me radius of the sphere instead of its volume, so I'm going to have to figure that out first," or "I need to know the speed of that train to be able to figure this out."

The third question is always important to keep in mind. It's framed the way it is for a reason. You have to assume that you already have the tool that is required to solve the math problem. You have to try to solve the problem using the tools that you know. Each and every concept you learn in math is a tool or shortcut to help you figure things out that you couldn't ordinarily figure. You have to know what tool you need to apply, but first you need to know that you've got to use your tools.

With the answers to these question firmly in mind, the word problem unravels. It transforms into a simple numbers problem.

If it can work while you're tutoring someone, it can certainly work while you're taking the test.

It takes familiarity and mastery in order to be able to quickly use the tools you've been given to solve the problems.

There is no math problem on the ACT or SAT that a student is not capable of answering. He or she just needs to have the tools of math.

Look at it this way. Do you remember a math test in elementary or middle school that was very challenging? What would it be like to take that test now? It would probably be pretty simple. That's because you've learned more since then.

You just have to learn math to a level beyond what they're testing on the ACT and SAT. Then you won't have any trouble with it. It is possible for the SAT to feel like taking a simple math test from yesteryear.

It's a question of whether you are ahead or behind. It's not a question of whether you have the innate ability or talent.

CRAIG GEHRING

Chapter 10
The Importance of Teaching

Like the rest of this book, this chapter is for you, not for your teacher.

One great way to improve your memory of your subject is to teach it. Learning grammar cements the concepts one way in your mind. Teaching grammar and explaining it forces you to see it all in a new light.

Very often you'll need to teach a subject or tutor someone in it before you can say that you've mastered it. It takes a deeper understanding of a subject to explain it rather than just learn it.

Often this deeper understanding is arrived at only once you try to teach it. The parts of it that you haven't quite worked out for yourself yet – you have to sort them out. You have to shake out what the most important parts of the subject are in teaching it. Often up until the point you need to help someone else know it, you won't know what those are.

This probably sounds pretty wild, but if you're having trouble with a subject, the best thing you could do is try to teach it.

Say, "I've got to teach Joe about this part of math tomorrow in class, so today I better figure out what the heck I'm doing."

You'll learn as you prepare and you'll learn again as you teach.

Teaching makes the subject grow three-dimensional. Your student challenges you and your subject in ways that you did not, yourself, challenge. It makes you grow strong in your subject.

If I wanted this to be a one-page book, I would say this:

The way to master the ACT and SAT is to pick up some of those SAT prep books and use them to tutor 10 people through every part of the test. Make their success wholly dependent upon your success as a teacher. And when you're not tutoring them, you work through the next day's lesson and figure out what you don't know how to teach. And at that point you'll be the SAT's master.

There's a lot more to it than that, but if I wanted to keep it to one page, that would be all she wrote.

Teaching makes it possible to understand a subject in a way that you otherwise can't. It creates a better web of information in your mind. Teaching is an intrinsic part of learning.

I'm sure you can remember a point where you had to tutor someone or give a presentation in class and you experienced this.

Not only is it a great feeling to help someone. You're also helping yourself.

Here is a trick. I am not trying to give you too many tricks because you have to keep them in mind all the time to use them and that's not very practical, but here is a helpful trick. Approach everything you learn from the standpoint that one day soon you might have to teach it. And if you don't understand it well enough to be able to teach it, then you need to ask more questions and learn more until you feel that you could teach it. If you can teach it, you've probably mastered it. But you won't hit the point of mastery unless you look at it from that angle.

Even something as simple as dribbling a basketball can be improved by looking at it from this viewpoint. If you want to do layups better, for instance, try teaching someone who doesn't know how to do it all. You'll probably be amazed how much better your own technique improves.

CRAIG GEHRING

CHAPTER 11
HOW MUCH READING IS ENOUGH?

We live in an under-read society. If you're the average American teen, you're more than likely horribly under-read.

Under-read is a word I think I made up that's the opposite of well-read. It isn't that you can't read. You just haven't read enough. I don't mean that as an insult. I just mean that it takes a certain amount of reading in order to be able to succeed in school, to have a level of literacy high enough to be able to easily grasp facts and improve your knowledge base.

It is possible to be well-read and not be a bookworm. But that being said, book worms do fare a lot better in school. And if you're behind and want to catch up, you might look an awful lot like a bookworm for a while until you've gotten enough reading under your belt.

One might say that someone who is highly intelligent likes to read more than the average Joe.

I think that the opposite is more likely true. Someone who likes to read more than the average Joe becomes highly intelligent.

I think students would do well to read at least five times as much as they are assigned in school.

The important thing here is to read at or below your reading level most of the time.

Any time you read a book over your reading level, it isn't as pleasurable. It becomes challenging, and not in a fun way.

One trick that really works is when you're ready to read something above your reading level (something that has words every few sentences that you're unfamiliar with), start with something highly entertaining. Something in a niche that's fascinating to you. This will balance out the challenge.

Although I hate to admit it, I received my first boost in reading level in elementary school because I was determined to understand a Nintendo game guide. The enjoyment I got out of the content kept me steadfastly reading and learning the words despite the challenge.

If your interest in reading wanes, you've probably picked up something too tough or too boring. Go back to the reading material you enjoyed.

A lot of it doesn't need to be on the particular subject you're studying. Reading in general will serve you well in mastering the SAT and ACT. Literacy plays a huge role in your ability to learn new things. I remind you again of the example of sitting in class and one out of every ten of the professor's words are in French. You'll understand a lot more in the class if you know French. That's one of the benefits of reading.

The other thing is that even if you know all of the rules of Grammar (which is a subject that can make or break you on the SAT and ACT) you won't do well in Grammar until you've read enough English to develop a sense of what sounds right and what sounds wrong. The better read you are, the better your grammar sense. It's like Spidey Sense, only it warns you against wrong answers instead of warning you against danger.

Reading is a habit. It can be rewarding. A steady diet of reading will serve you well. Reading is like the concept of "Reserve Miles". I've never met a steady reader who really had much trouble in school.

There are books that you can read that can give you a particular advantage in certain subjects. More on this in another chapter. But suffice to say that first you need to read a LOT of books. Fiction, non-fiction, the more the better.

CHAPTER 12
USING CLASS TIME

I'm sure you've had the thought while reading all of this, "This sounds like I can't have a life!"

Nothing could be further from the truth.

Actually, once you've gotten to the head of the class, you have plenty of time. School is easily and quickly taken care of.

And there is one often neglected source of time that many students ignore: class time.

Try this exercise. Whenever you have a spare minute in a class (because you're finished with the assignment, or there's nothing else to do, etc.) pick up the textbook for the class and start reading it. Whenever your teacher lets you goof off, pick up your homework for another class and get it done.

You'll be amazed how little homework you're left with when you get home. And you'll also be way ahead of the class in little time.

There is a ton of untapped down time that you can use to your advantage. If you only applied the principles in this book during your class time, you could make it work.

Of course, if you're really pursuing mastery – if you've gotten to the point where you're enjoying learning and the benefits it brings – you won't just limit your education to class time.

Another part about class time: make the most of your teachers' lectures. Actually listen to what they're saying and participate.

You'll get the most benefit out of what they say if you've already read about it. Just being a few days ahead in the text will result in their lectures being reviews instead of confusing first introductions to the concepts.

You are wasting your class time if your teacher is lecturing on a book that you were supposed to read but haven't yet.

As you gradually get ahead of the class through your own reading, the teachers' lectures will make a lot more sense and be more memorable. They'll punch the high points that they're going to test on, and you'll actually remember what they say. Then instead of you having to spend your time studying for the test coming up, you'll just remember the concept they already went over.

If you've ever had the experience of a teacher talking about something you'd already learned, you know what I mean. She covers some new points, or emphasizes something differently, but you're familiar enough with the subject that you can remember what has been said. You're not wading through the subject for the first time in confusion. You've already done that and now you're into a neat review.

Ideally, you should feel like the teacher is reviewing the subject for you. You should feel like you can raise your hand and answer all of their questions. You should not be so beaten down by all these new facts in this newly introduced subject that you can't track with the teacher and understand what's going on.

At some point in this process of using your class time correctly, the teacher may recognize that you're way ahead and begin to tell you not to worry about these particular assignments. He may give you more advanced lessons instead. And as long as these are making sense, and you're able to go it alone, take advantage of this. Continue to use the class time to pursue mastering your education.

If you don't get ahead of what they are teaching to the average student in high school, you will not score much higher than the average high school student on the SAT and ACT tests.

Don't be afraid of getting ahead. Embrace it. And use getting ahead as an opportunity to get even further ahead, unencumbered!

CHAPTER 13
GRAMMAR, OR WHAT SOUNDS RIGHT

The key to scoring well in the grammar and composition sections of the ACT and SAT is being familiar with the language.

When you're familiar with English, you write in full, correct sentences. You're able to fully develop your ideas in writing. And you are able to identify almost all grammar and composition errors when you see them.

You're able to do this not because you have memorized a bunch of crazy rules (although you do know the rules). You're able to do this because you've read enough correct English and heard enough correct English that you can identify problems when they exist.

A musician can hear when an instrument or voice is off key. Likewise you can hear when something isn't being related correctly in the English language, but only if you're exposed to a lot of it.

Two of the "holy books" mentioned in this book will help you develop this skill further. But these books will be relatively worthless to you unless you're familiar with English already.

The more you read and the more you write, the better you'll be able to perform in the grammar section.

While it appears to be true that all you have to do is memorize the grammar rules, the real way to blow this section out of the water is to read and write a good bit.

How much is a good bit? Probably five times more than what you're actually assigned in school, for starters.

If you only do what you're assigned in school, you'll have an average performance. If you want an average performance on the ACT, SAT, in school and in life, there's no reason to read this book.

So in addition to learning all the grammar rules and reviewing the "holy books," you need to just read and write a ton. Read and write on what you're interested in.

Take the opportunities when you get them to help proofread your classmates' essays and school assignments. This is great practice and will also help you turn a critical eye to your own writing material.

There is a trend in school to critique all the grammar errors in a student's essay. While this is all fine and well, the only way someone learns to write correctly is to write a lot and read a lot.

Quantity results in quality. If you write twenty essays all slightly wrong, your grammar and composition abilities will still be much better than someone who writes only one essay and works all year on perfecting it.

Teachers would do well to get their students to write an essay each day trying to convey some concept they believe or something they want to tell others about.

If your teacher doesn't have you do this, you would do well to find something to write about and spend a little time each day writing about it.

You can't tell if you're off key if you never sing and you never hear anyone else sing. You can't have good grammar and composition skills without a lot of reading and writing under your belt.

CRAIG GEHRING

Chapter 14
When Should You Get Tutoring?

One thing that has always puzzled me is the obsession with classroom settings nationwide.

If students are underperforming on their standardized tests, the administrative solution by the Department of Education and the school districts seems to be to make system-wide changes in curriculum and teacher selection.

Actually what needs to be done is that each individual student needs to be picked up in small groups or solo and tutored through the materials that they don't understand. Each student needs to be tested for deficiencies and then caught up.

This wouldn't be homework help tutoring. This would be actually making "academic repair", patching up the problem areas in the child's education.

It is actually impossible for a teacher in a classroom setting to catch a student up who is two grade levels behind in reading. That simply doesn't happen. Even if the student works as hard as every other student in the class, he or she will be two grade levels behind every year until tutoring or remediation happens.

The point here is that if you are behind or having trouble in a subject area, get a tutor. Don't get a tutor that's just going to walk you through your homework. Get a tutor that is going to diagnose what you missed and help you to understand it.

If a student is behind in reading level, one of the best things you could do for him is to get him to read aloud to you, and help him to understand anything that he didn't quite understand. You'll boost his vocabulary by helping him to understand the definitions of words that he didn't know the meaning of, and by getting him through a volume of material.

In doing this, make sure you're reading things that are at or close to his reading level. You'll know that you're reading the right material if he or she doesn't have too much trouble with it, and when you ask questions, he or she can show an understanding of what's going on in the book. Read things the student is interested in.

Parents would do well to do this with their kids.

If you'd like to raise your grades and score highly on college readiness tests like the ACT and SAT, read aloud to your parents every day until such time that you feel comfortable just reading on your own and looking up the words in dictionaries.

Recognize that everyone needs a teacher. You can accomplish a lot studying on your own, but it helps to have someone else there, too, who is familiar with the subject or at a higher level of reading to help you understand.

Likewise, don't pass up an opportunity to tutor someone. An opportunity to educate is an opportunity to learn.

Chapter 15
The "Holy Books"

There are a few books that are amazing that I highly recommend to you. They are fundamental books that will give you a deeper understanding of math and English.

I call them the "holy books" because they can help you all out of proportion to the amount of time you have to invest in studying them.

Amongst people who are specialists in journalism, or math, they're held in a sort of awe that causes people to whisper their names.

I was lucky enough to have heard of them.

They are:

The Elements of Style by William Strunk & E.B. White

The Elements of Grammar by Margaret D. Shertzer

and

The Art of Problem Solving by Sandor Lehoczky & Richard Rusczyk

These are well-kept secrets that will boost your scores.

I daresay that just reading these books cover to cover will improve your scores on the ACT and SAT and improve your performance in school immeasurably.

They are simple and they are relatively easy to read.

Get someone to help you with them if you have questions or difficulty wrapping your mind around a particular concept.

These books reinforce and give you a new angle on subjects you've already been studying.

I'm sure there are other books out there that are like this. These are the ones I've found are the best. They're all thin, easy reads to get through. Don't ignore them. If you only have one week to prep for the test, pick up these books and just give them a read through.

Chapter 16
The Importance of Winning (and Losing)

A good friend of mine runs a non-profit inner city tutoring center. She had an 8th grade student who was old enough to be in high school who actually tested at a 4th grade level across the boards.

Upon enrolling him in her program, she had a big decision to make. The kid was extremely combative, obviously suffering from self-esteem issues, and she was worried that if she put him in the appropriate small group academically, that the first day would be the last day she ever saw him.

She stuck to her guns. He spent his first day in a small group with students five and six years younger than him.

At the end of the tutoring session, the kid was grinning ear to ear. He told his tutor that for the first time ever, he could do this.

The road to mastery of a subject is a path of steadily winning. If you always lose, if you never understand, you're never going to make it.

Part of the reason why people start losing on the road to mastery is that they don't recognize how much better they can get at something. And so they move on to something that they can't do at all.

If I had doggedly kept trying to play the Chili Peppers song on guitar without any of the intermediate steps, I would have kept losing and eventually quit guitar.

But if I had learned how to "kind of" play a chord, and never really done it over and over again until I mastered it, I would have started losing as well and eventually quit.

Once you can do something, you've only started to win. Now it's time to get better and better and better.

Once you learn how to do a layup in basketball, for instance, have you mastered it? Have you won all you could? No. Now let's try to do three layups in a row. Now five. Now ten. Now let's do twenty layups and not miss a single one. Now let's do layups while someone is guarding you a little. Now let's make it tougher. And you win all the way.

The way to lose is to say, "Now I can do one layup every once in a while. So now I'll join a league of basketball players twice my age and really have fun."

To have a skill and to master a skill are two entirely different things. Bite off more than you can chew and you start losing, simple as that. It doesn't matter how good you are, you can always bite off more than you can chew.

Losing is a dangerous thing. Continue to lose and you may start to accept mediocrity. You may lower your expectations of yourself. That's a slippery slope. Once you start lowering expectations, the only answer to your own failures becomes to further lower your expectations.

The easiest way to begin lowering your expectations is to start with your expectations too high.

By all means shoot for the stars. But figure out where the stairs to the stars are, and walk one step at a time. Always expect of yourself the next step. Don't expect to just appear in the stars in five minutes. That's a sure way to end up stuck on the ground.

Part of winning is having a winning mentality. You get that by winning. Once you start winning, you don't want to stop. You become more willing to push yourself, to stay on top of your game. Lose too much and you lose your winning mentality.

The way to regain a winning mentality is to do what you've already won at. If you're getting frustrated playing guitar, pick up that drill exercise that you're already great at it and run through it ten more times. Do it a little faster. You're winning again.

If you read a book a little above your reading level, and you're doing great, don't go diving off into the encyclopedia next. Pick up another book at the same level, by the same author, even, and read that. You'll notice you read it a little faster than the previous one, and got a little more out of it. Read ten more. Then go for something a little tougher.

Having a winning attitude is important in the field of education because in order to learn anything you have to actively learn. You have to work at it and ask questions and research and find out. All of these things take your own effort and your own desire. If you are losing, or feel that you have lost, it will be hard or impossible to actively learn. You'll feel stuck and you'll feel like quitting.

One way to regain your winning attitude is to go back to a lesson that you did pretty well in. Find more questions or problems like the ones you already did. Go through them and answer them. Get perfect at it. Get to where you can go faster and faster. Then come back to what you're having trouble with. Find the part of it that you can understand.

Get help. Break down the trouble area.

It will be a lot easier from the winning side. This is just straight psychology. It works.

There is another side of this. Losing is important, too, provided that you understand how this works.

As a matter of fact, mastering any subject or moving to the head of any class or activity requires you to lose some. You start at the bottom and through experience and education you move to the top.

Once you're the best or close to the best, you have to move to a tougher group, a higher class, a bigger challenge. Sure, that's great that you're the best at junior track. Now it's time to move up to varsity.

When you start, you'll get torn to bits. You'll lose. The people that you're working with will be in better shape, will be smarter, will know more about your subject area or activity. That's why you're moving up. And if you keep these principles in mind, you'll eventually move up, too.

There are plenty of actors that stay in their hometown and are known as the "best actor in Chesapeake," or what have you. But some of these guys move to Hollywood and fight to get to the top of the stack. And the winners are the best of the best. Even then, the best try to move up into higher circles.

You can improve your ability just by surrounding yourself with people who are more proficient than you. You might lose for a while. But when you go back and visit the group or class that you were a part of, you'll notice a big difference in your skills.

Don't be afraid to take on a new challenge just because you're afraid of losing.

But don't forget that the only way to mastery is to win, little by little. Don't bite off more than you can chew, but for God's sake, keep biting!

CHAPTER 17
ROUNDING AN EDUCATION

An education isn't a collection of bullet points and flash cards. It's a body of knowledge.

By reading and learning about what interests you, and constantly expanding the scope of your horizons, the lessons that you're assigned in school will be easier.

A rounded education, you could say, is one where you've filled in all the blanks between the bullet points and flash cards with your own reading and study and History Channel watching.

If you don't take charge of rounding your own education, at as early a point as possible, school might give you some difficulties. And the ACT and SAT certainly will.

I was reading last year about a Buddhist principle of thought. It was talking about how before every action, there is a thought or desire. For example, someone wouldn't be violent towards another person unless, before that, he had violence in his heart or mind. It was talking about how one might meditate in order to cleanse one's mind of such thoughts, so as to improve one's actions.

Now I am not a Buddhist and probably I did not grasp this perfectly, so my apologies if I got this wrong, but the point is interesting enough. Your thoughts and attitudes definitely change how you act.

Before you go tearing off *doing* the actions talked about in this book – which will mainly involve you *actively studying and mastering* and probably reading a lot more than you used to – you'll need to find an attitude or thought which makes this possible.

There is a spark in each of us that loves to learn, that loves to make progress towards our goals. In order to enjoy learning, you have to reach that spark. You have to rationalize for yourself how learning these things is going to help you to do what you love and to become successful in reaching the goals that you hold dear for your own life.

If you figure this out, the studying will be easy. The actions of studying and actively learning and reading are only byproducts of your curiosity and desire to learn remaining intact.

Chapter 18
Memory and Repetition

Repetition and review are the keys to remembering facts.

If you can't remember something, you can't really say that you know it. So unless you remember facts after you've studied them, they aren't a part of your body of knowledge. Sure, you have the right to say, "I studied algebra in high school." But you couldn't say that you knew algebra unless you remembered it.

Don't expect to do well on any test if the first time you see the information is the night before the test. But if the first time you see the info is right before the test, be sure to take the time to read it over and over again. And then test yourself on what you know, over and over again.

You'll do much, much better for a test on Friday to split up your review time. Study some the Friday before. On Tuesday, pick it up again and review it all. Then on Thursday night, review it again. The studying will be a lot easier and you'll do a lot better on the test.

This has to do with how the mind works.

In the advertising world, it's a known fact that advertising doesn't have an effect on anybody until people have seen the ad at least a dozen times.

If you can't remember that Wheaties help you have a good morning without seeing it a dozen times, then don't expect to remember the year Benedict Arnold betrayed our country after just reading it once.

Just like the advertisements we see are drowned out by other advertisements, the facts that we try to learn are drowned out by other facts.

Repetition and review will help you remember anything.

Ask a musician how many times she has repeated a song that she is good at, and you'll have an excellent illustration of this concept. Ask a basketball player how many layups he has practiced in his life.

The SAT and ACT are similar to midterms in that you are quizzed on a variety of topics and skills that you've learned over a long period of time. So ideally in your preparation for the ACT and SAT, you go over the test material a few times: a year before, six months before, three months before, a month before, a week before, etc.

In any subject, you would do well to spend a little time each month reviewing what you've already learned, picking up anything you may have forgotten or let slip by quizzing yourself on some of the concepts. Just a little bit of this can help you cement all of the information in your mind and keep you from having a nightmare of a cramming session the day before midterms or the ACT and SAT.

CHAPTER 19
OVERSTIMULATION AND INSTANT GRATIFICATION

I was reading some writing tips a few years ago and I encountered a fascinating writing quote by Sir Arthur Conan Doyle. He was the prolific writer of the Sherlock Holmes series, among others. He basically said that in order to write, he found it necessary to first remove all other distractions. He said that he had to remove from his environment everything that was better to him than writing. And then he could get down to the business of writing.

What struck me is that someone who obviously wrote a ton still had to isolate himself from distractions before he could get down to business.

In other words, there were activities, such as hanging out with friends, going to shows, etc. that were better in his mind than writing, and as long as he could engage in those he didn't write.

In today's society, there are all manner of things that are far more stimulating than learning. As a matter of fact, we could say that American culture has developed such highly refined methods of entertainment that people spend an inordinate amount of time being entertained, on average.

One of the purposes of the mind is to seek pleasure and avoid pain. It is possible, I think, for something to be so pleasant on the short term (instant gratification) that it overrides any concern for the long term. Even when logic would indicate that one shouldn't watch *American Idol* before the big test the next morning, how many people can resist?

It's almost as though our ability to entertain has outstripped our brain's evolution in terms of its abilities to identify what is good and bad for ourselves.

Overstimulation is a major problem today. It can actually stand in the way of applying the principles of this book. If the trend of over-stimulation continues, we could have a lot more problems ahead of us for this nation.

I believe that it's possible for modern entertainment to be so thor-oughly enjoyable and stimulating to the brain that people will actually prefer the instant gratification of receiving it rather than engaging less stimulating and pleasurable activities that actually improve your ability to have a successful future.

Our society was much better read and more highly literate when reading a book was one of the staples of home entertainment.

You see this all the time in entertainment addicts. Internet addicts, Facebook addicts, TV addicts, news addicts, gaming addicts. Holly-wood has highly refined the process of entertainment. Watch a modern sitcom. Notice they're able to make the audience laugh every five or ten seconds. This is science. They make a fortune for it. America has fig-ured out how to bottle pleasure.

Spend a little time watching the news. Notice how riveting it's made to be. Watch a TV series. They have it down how to hook you. You can watch episode after episode after episode.

Not every human being is interested in the same thing. They have that figured out, too. Surveys and focus groups help them to find your interests, and they make a fascinating show about that.

It's so GOOD that your mind says, "This is the thing to watch. This is the thing to do!" And I'm not saying your mind is wrong. But I am saying that in the presence of this box that magically serves out wonderful, bottled happiness from the airwaves, you're going to have a hard time maintaining your interest in your studies.

This may be a blessing in disguise. It means that if you really understand this principle of overstimulation, and take actions to counteract it, you could move to the head of the class very quickly. Your classmates are too distracted to keep up.

I'm not saying no TV, no Facebook, no gaming, etc., etc. That's not my point. I'm just pointing out a phenomenon here.

You'll see it most clearly when you make yourself unplug for a week. You'll start to get terribly bored. And it will be several days before the thoughts of turning on the TV or checking your Facebook get filled instead with thoughts of seeking things that are much less pleasurable, but still enjoyable. Like reading.

The average American's diet of information could be likened to a child who only eats sugar and candy. The child who eats only sugar or candy would never dream of eating anything more substantial. It's not interesting enough. Only this sugar and candy doesn't make him sick. It only makes him want more. Only by kicking the habit of sugary foods and drinks would the child begin to gain interest in Macaroni and Cheese and McDonald's Happy Meals and other fine American dishes.

I am a gifted child, you could say. My intelligence is higher than most. But I can't tell you how much time of my life I have wasted on gaming. Just being honest with you. I would be studying something on a computer and become irresistibly drawn to playing a computer game.

It was only during periods of time that I had pulled myself away from that did I really learn or get things done or get ahead.

You have the benefit of not being able to do these things so much in school. But if you're on a steady diet of bottled, meaningless enter-tainment from the moment you get home from school 'til the time you go to sleep (or even not so drastic) school will be something to survive through, not something to get an education from.

If gaming is your thing, you'd do best to find something that helps you learn at the same time. I actually benefited a great deal from the old computer game *Mario's Time Machine*, which is a thinly veiled history lesson.

If TV is your thing, perhaps the History Channel is something for you to look at. I'm not saying that every moment of your life should be an educational experience. But bottled happiness is a trap that the majority of Americans have fallen into. And if you have fallen into it yourself, if you try to follow the recommendations of your book, it will feel like torture. It will feel like being force-fed steak when all you want is a pack of Skittles.

Drugs overwhelm the pleasure receptors of the brain. Modern en-tertainment does this to a slight degree. In my opinion, that's why we start seeing these new mental illnesses popping up having to do with Internet addiction. Long before there was Internet addiction, there was TV addiction, although the malady is so widespread that you could hardly call it a disease. I read somewhere that the average American watches at least 6 hours of television per day.

The harm of this is not really just in the time lost from watching television, etc. It's really in what it does to your thinking process and your perceptions the other 10 hours you're not sleeping.

It's the pleasure of study, the AHAs! and the Wows! and the I Didn't Know Thats! that keep you going and get you ahead. It is possible to be completely numb to this if your entertainment diet is off the Richter scale.

Telling yourself, "Okay, I get through this page of study, then I get to watch my show," doesn't work. The reason is that this isn't the attitude you need to have while learning. If you are trying to get through it to go on to something more interesting, you are just receiving (at best). You aren't actively learning. There's no way for you to be able to build a body of knowledge like that. You'll be approaching building your education with the same attitude as you would doing the laundry.

Unplugging is an exercise I've had to do many, many times in my life. Even though I'm writing this, I don't want you to think I'm getting up on a high horse. I had to unplug from canned entertainment very recently. One of the fruits of that was this book. But while I'm on a diet of steady entertainment, I don't write very much, and I'm definitely not on top of my game. You can know all this and still be hooked.

All I am asking is that you should try unplugging. Writhe through the boredom. And see what happens. You'll be surprised how productive and how inquisitive you naturally are once you've turned off all the noise.

In the short run, you'll have more fun sticking with the media. But in the long term, there is nothing better than being ahead of the curve, successful in whatever field you decide to tackle in life. There's nothing more pleasurable than being excellent, than being the one in the spotlight rather than the one watching the guys in the spotlight. The road getting there isn't as fun, but once you're there, you'll never want to go back.

Of course, it's not just the TV and the computer that are at fault. I've met plenty of people who are hooked on romance novels or that next Grisham novel. The publishing industry is no dummy, and has to refine its science of entertainment constantly to keep up with TV and the movies. That being said, at least when you're reading, you're improving your literacy.

So if you feel you need to taper yourself down from twelve hours of TV, pick up *Harry Potter* or *Twilight* or something. But when you're really off the diet, you'll be amazed how enjoyable non-fiction is.

If you're having a hard time swallowing this, if you think I'm probably mental, that's just more evidence that you need to try unplugging at least once.

My first clue into this was the mental clarity and natural creativity I would gain whenever I'd go off for a week to a camping trip or a church retreat. I was unplugged, through no choice of my own, and when I came back home (if I didn't immediately dive to my Nintendo) I was actively learning a lot more and moving ahead in life.

For other people, it's talking on the phone. It's hanging out with the girlfriend. It's drugs. It's alcohol. Different strokes for different folks. The point is that *overstimulation and instant gratification can be detrimental to your ability to learn and get ahead in life.*

Stimulation is different than overstimulation. Overstimulation makes it hard for you to find enjoyment out of life. If you can't enjoy studying and learning, you absolutely will not learn.

I am sure some of you reading this are saying to yourselves, "Wow, this guy is recommending that I have a lame life."

That's not my intention. Just try it. Try unplugging for a week or two. Stay unplugged until you aren't constantly wanting to plug back in. Let it ride until you've gone a day without even thinking about diving into canned entertainment. And then survey how different your life is.

I could simplify this instead of getting so philosophical.

The entertainment scene in America gives you the perfect opportunity to get ahead in life.

If everyone is running a marathon, but only running a couple hours each day, you can win just by running a couple hours extra.

In other words, cut a couple hours out of your media diet and replace it with learning something, and you'll win the marathon every time.

It's so simple, it's cheating. And it works.

It is impossible for someone to achieve mastery on a steady diet of overstimulation and instant gratification.

Chapter 20
Quick Testing Tricks

If you skipped to this chapter, let me tell you I totally understand. I would have done the same thing. The point of this book isn't to give you some quick test-taking tricks. It's to help you master the ACT or SAT, and to give you the keys to mastering education overall.

That being said, if you use these tips, you'll probably score an extra point or two on the ACT (or 50 – 100 points or so on the SAT), even if this is all you apply out of the whole book.

Focus

Taking the SAT and the ACT can be likened to picking an apple tree. You get points based on how many apples that you pick. In the higher point ranges (over 1400 in the SAT and over 32 in the ACT) a single answer can make a significant difference on what you end up scoring.

The ACT and SAT are both timed tests. You're let loose on the apple tree and you have a certain amount of time to pick as many apples as possible.

Your preparation determines how far up the apple tree you can climb, and how quickly you can move. But it's your focus that helps you to find all the apples you can at the level that you're at.

The key test taking skill is the ability to focus.

Many people do poorly on the ACT and the SAT because they can't get through the test. The reason they can't get through the test is that they cannot focus.

These test questions are usually arranged randomly as to difficulty. They don't go from easiest to hardest, front to back.

So part of focusing is asking yourself these questions: "Do I know how to answer this question? Do I know how to answer it quickly?" If not, move on. You can go back to it later. You need to pick all the apples you can easily pick before you try to go any higher.

The worst thing that can happen is to have five questions in the back of the test that you could have answered easily but never got to.

When you read a question that you don't understand, confusion follows. It clouds your mind. Focus lets you clear your mind and go on to the next question.

Most schools provide the PSAT for practice before you take the real thing. If you didn't get all the way through the PSAT, you should take practice ACT and SAT tests using a timer until you can focus enough to get through the whole thing.

This is just a matter of speed and focus. It's not a question of whether you can answer all the questions. It's just a question of whether you are familiar enough with the "tree" and have practiced focusing enough to get all the way around it and pick all the "low hanging fruit".

When students say that they are bad test takers, what they are really trying to say is that they either aren't prepared, or have trouble focusing.

Test taking is a skill like any other. To master it, you have to do it again and again, and work on developing specific skills as you practice. The key skill here is focus.

Focus means the ability to control your own attention and direct it to the task at hand. It's hard to keep your attention directed if you're in over your head in a test. But it can be done. And the priority of your focus needs to be finding questions that you can answer.

I was totally prepared for the ACT and SAT and still I skipped a few questions and came back to them later. The answer wasn't coming to me, and I knew I would need to rack my brain to figure it out. So I kept my focus and continued answering questions, then doubled back.

Time is of the Essence

Time is tight on the ACT and SAT. They do not give you generous portions of time. If you don't keep this in mind, you won't get the score you deserve.

Time is a major factor. The tests are finding out how well you know this information *within a tight timeframe.* It's best to get familiar with the time frame by answering practice tests under a time limit. It's a lot less time than you really need to answer everything comfortably.

When they give you the test and get ready to tell you to start, you should feel like you're at the starting line of a race, ready for the gun to go off. And when the gun fires, start working that test as fast as you can. Speeding through the questions you are certain of will give you time at the end of the testing segment to go back, answer any tricky ones, and verify that you've answered correctly, got everything in the right blank, etc.

Take advantage of the part of the test that you're certain of, the easy questions, to get a leg up on time. Go as fast as you can while still maintaining accuracy.

Making a dedicated effort to go *faster* will get you some extra points. Speed allows for more time, and more time allows for more quality.

Develop the ability to recognize a question that will take you a long time.

Also, develop the ability to recognize a question that you simply cannot figure out. This is different than a question that will take you a long time, because in the end you spend all the time on it but don't even get any points for it.

WATCH OUT FOR "THE BLANK"

"The blank" is the deadly monster that will kill you on any timed test. The blank is the point you hit while reading a passage or a math problem where your mind has completely spaced out. You are suddenly thinking of something else than the test, or you're thinking of nothing at all.

You have to recognize that you've hit a blank spot.

Sometimes a blank spot can occur when you've hit something confusing. The key to beating a blank is to direct your own attention. Basically when you've hit a blank spot, you've hit something so confusing or boring or what have you that you are no longer controlling your own attention, even though you're in the middle of a testing environment.

The solution is simple. Focus your attention on *something*.

Once you recognize that you've gone blank, you can do a number of things to focus. One simple thing is to skip to the test questions about the passage and start understanding those. Then go back to the passage.

Another thing you can do is just skip to another section and come back.

You can go back a couple paragraphs and try reading again.

But whatever you do, don't just keep staring blankly at that segment of the passage. And don't keep "reading," meaning having your eyes scan down the page without you having any clue what's being said. (You'd be amazed how many people do this.) As soon as you recognize that you've gone blank, take control.

Spotting French

Earlier in this book I mentioned how if you run across words that you don't understand fully in your studies, it's a bit akin to having random French words instead of English words in your lessons. These words you don't understand can be a cause of going blank.

One trick that really works at lowering how many times you go blank is to underline any word you're not sure of as you read along. It has the effect of you instantly maintaining your focus by directing your attention after running across something that isn't understood. It can also help you identify a problem area, because in some cases the meaning of the word will determine an answer to a question, and knowing that it's French to you will help you skip it and go on to something you're more sure of. That way you can also go back to it and use context clues and your understanding the parts of the word to figure out what they're trying to say.

SKIP

I've already said it in just about every section of this chapter. If you're not sure how to answer something quickly, skip it and come back later. Put a star next to the question number on your answer sheet, and go back to the stars when you've gotten through the whole test section.

If you want to be real fancy, put two stars next to questions that you have no clue on. That way you can go back to the one-stars and finish them before you mess with the two-stars.

If you aren't willing to skip questions, you're not recognizing the fact that the distribution of easy questions is spread throughout the entire test. You get the same number of points for answering an easy question correctly as answering a hard question. So if you give hard questions undue amounts of time, you will be penalized.

THE PROCESS OF ELIMINATION

The process of elimination is something that's mentioned in every ACT and SAT prep book, and it bears repeating.

Getting a right answer earns you points. But eliminating wrong answers ultimately earns you points as well.

If you could just eliminate all the answers on the test that you knew were wrong, and then guessed randomly amongst the right ones, you would earn points on the ACT and SAT. You wouldn't do great, but the point is that eliminating wrong answers improves your score.

So eliminating wrong answers is definitely a part of any multiple choice test.

The SAT even penalizes completely random guesses. But if you can eliminate a couple wrong answers, and then guess between what's left, statistically you'll still win.

The way to eliminate answers is to plug them in. If they don't make sense or don't work, they are definitely not the answer.

X-marks on the wrong answers can help you focus on your remaining possibilities.

Plug In the Answers

Another take on the process of elimination is useful not only in math but in reading, English, and grammar as well.

Plug in each answer and see if it makes sense. The one that works is your answer. Some math questions are quite difficult, but if there are only five possible answers they become quite easy.

Plug in the number they give you for the X, or plug in the segment they give you as the replacement for the reading section. See if it works.

This involves a lot less thinking and calculation and can save you a ton of time and heartache.

There will be questions that you have no idea how to solve that you can still test the answers on and find the right one.

I actually solved several of the math and English questions on my test this way not because I couldn't work it out or was stuck but because it was faster.

So you can use the "plug it in" method not only to identify wrong answers but to identify the correct answers as well.

SIMILARITIES IN ANSWER CHOICES

Put yourself in the shoes of the test writer for a moment. He has to use multiple choices to discern whether or not you know how to solve a problem.

To do this he has to provide you with opportunities to trip up. That's because if there is only one answer that's even close to the correct option, then when you calculate the problem out you'll know whether or not you've gotten it right, and will keep trying until you come up with one of the multiple choices.

So what the test writer does is solve the problem, and provide answers that would typically come up if you made an error somewhere along the line.

That way, when you make an error, you get the same "answer" as an option on the test, you bubble that option and get it wrong!

Tricky test writers! But you can use this fact to your advantage.

All other things being equal, if you are just randomly guessing at a test answer, you can eliminate choices that are completely different than the rest of the choices. For example:

a. .001

b. -.001

c. .0001

d. 43

e. -7

Statistically speaking, you can eliminate choices D and E.

Now this isn't always true. The reason why this isn't always true is that the test writers are aware that some students can detect this, and so sometimes will create similar choices, none of which are right. But all things being equal, it's a better guess to go with the similar choices.

From there you're able to eliminate some of your options. For example, in this test question, if you know that your answer has to be negative, a good guess would be B, even if you had no idea how to answer the test question beyond that!

This is a weak clue compared to actually plugging things in and using the process of elimination. But it's better than nothing at all. And it can actually help you get a few extra questions right!

NONE OF THE ABOVE

You have to be careful with this one. As a rule, any time I come up with None of the Above, I check it twice. Or if I'm racing against time, I star it and come back to it and verify.

The reason for this is that if you come up with an answer, and this answer is one of the multiple choices available, then that's an affirmation that you probably got it right.

When you come up with an answer that's different than any of the choices available, you get no such affirmation, even if "None of the Above" is an option. So I'm always careful and double check it to make sure I got it right. If it's a math problem, verify that you've done all your math operations right, that you've got it in the correct unit (feet instead of inches, for instance), that you're actually answering the question and not accidentally solving the wrong thing. If you get the same answer again after checking all of these things, go with "None of the Above". But you'll be surprised how many times you catch yourself in a mistake.

The people who write the test will throw in the choice "None of the Above" quite a bit, but only sometimes will that be the correct answer. Otherwise people would know to just bubble in "None of the Above" whenever they see it on the test!

DOES IT SOUND RIGHT?

This is yet another variation of plugging in the answers. Take each multiple choice and plug it in to the Reading or Grammar segment. Does it sound right?

Also, if you are having trouble figuring out whether something "sounds right," or "looks right," it helps to ignore all of the dependent clauses that are in the sentence but aren't actually being asked about. This helps to cancel out some of the noise.

For example, in this sentence:

The quick brown fox, who on this day was just eating five sandwiches, and contemplating jumping many creeks, <u>were</u> happy to see the sun peek through the clouds.

For the purposes of figuring out whether "were" is the correct word in that sentence, and adjusting it to the correct word, you can take out all the dependent clauses that don't go with the subject and verb you're working on. So in this example you could ignore "who on this day was just eating five sandwiches, and contemplating jumping many creeks…"

You're left with this:

The quick brown fox <u>were</u> happy to see the sun part.

This is a simpler problem to solve. In this example it's obvious that your subject is singular but your verb is plural, so the verb should be *was*. This trick can help you dissect more complicated grammar problems as well.

In trying to work out a grammar question, say the paragraph aloud in your head, or whisper it to yourself. Chances are, the answer that sounds right is the correct option.

This is especially true if you've followed my recommendations on reading *Elements of Style* and *Elements of Grammar*. You'll have a good sense of this.

GUESS

The instructions in the SAT make it very clear that you'll be penalized for guessing.

What they don't say is that you get penalized as well for not guessing!

Statistically, if you're able to eliminate all but two or three of the answers, taking your best guess from there is actually the way to go.

If you answer incorrectly, you lose a little. But if you don't answer at all, you're giving away the points.

On the ACT, you're not penalized for guessing. While you're taking the ACT, bubble in an answer to every question, even when you skip it with a star. The reason for this is that leaving blank answers will kill your score. You will score lower than someone just as good as you who guessed instead of leaving blanks.

You can get caught with the timer going off and blank questions still there.

If you end up not knowing the answer to twenty questions on the ACT, by guessing you'll get four or five right that you wouldn't have gotten.

FOOD AND REST

Part of focus is being rested and eating properly. This can't start the night before the test. Saying, "I'm going to go to sleep early tonight before the test," usually won't work because your body is in a certain rhythm. You'll end up lying there, not going to sleep, then actually falling asleep even later than before.

You should start going to sleep early and sleeping until you're really rested at least a week before the test.

You'll be amazed at the clarity of mind you achieve just from being fully rested. Being rested has a huge bearing on your focus, your speed, and your accuracy.

Likewise, eating properly can help a lot. A few weeks before the test, make sure you're eating veggies and plenty of protein. I say that because those are the things commonly dropped out of the food pyramid in an American diet. Just follow that FDA food pyramid, or plate, or whatever our governmental agencies are using to encourage good eating nowadays. And stay away from an excess of sugary foods and caffeine.

If you haven't had any caffeine for a few weeks, a cup of coffee or tea can help right before you take the test. I'm not pushing drugs here – but in the short term a little caffeine can definitely speed up your mental process.

Likewise, nothing contributes to hitting blank spots or getting sleepy in the test like sugar or carbs. Stay away from these the morning before the test. A bunch of biscuits or pancakes drenched in honey or syrup is not the ideal breakfast before the test. Probably best would be eggs and bacon and a bit of toast – or the vegetarian equivalent if you're a vegetarian.

CERTAINTY

Some people know the answer but still agonize over whether they should bubble it in.

They are killing their scores.

If you fall into this category, you need to practice knowing when you're right.

Get a practice test and figure out a problem. Then instead of agonizing over it, bubble it in and then look up the answer.

Chances are you got it right.

You'll learn to trust your instincts.

Every second you spend on a question you already figured out is stealing from the time you can spend to answer the other questions.

It's better to figure everything out one time than to figure out half the test twice. You have to have certainty going into the test. You have to be certain of what you know how to do, and you also have to have certainty in what you don't know how to do (so that you can skip to what you do know!)

Epilogue
How to Read This Book:
The Beginning Last

Use a few of these tips and you'll score a little better.

I hope for some of you this book makes the difference. I hope it helps you to get a scholarship or get into that school you've been shooting for. If it does, please email me and let me know. I'd love to hear about it. My contact info is in the back of this book.

I hope in reading this you picked up the secret.

Your path to excelling in life begins with a decision. That decision has a few parts to it.

You have to make up your mind that you can succeed, and you have to make up your mind that you will succeed.

Work that out for yourself, and you'll have won half the battle.

From there you can work out what you're going to succeed at, and how.

I hope that this book helps you a little in doing that. There's a lot more to life than an ACT or SAT score. An education doesn't make you ready for those tests. It helps you to get ready for life.

Your education is in your hands. Good luck!

Acknowledgments

Special thanks to my wife, Brittany, my mom, Lisa, my entire family, and everyone who has been a part of my educational journey. Many thanks are due to Bobbie Clark, the most dedicated educator I've ever met. Also thanks to the staff at Ring Marketing for doing such a great job holding down the fort and making it possible to have the time to complete this project. And of course thanks to my editor, Michael Laird.

About the Author

Craig Gehring has helped thousands of students work toward their higher ed dreams since 2003, his junior year in high school when he earned perfect scores on both the ACT and the SAT. That year, parents started calling in to the school, asking him to tutor their children. Ten years later, Gehring has written the book, literally, on mastering the ACT and leads an effort to improve preparation for standardized tests. His *ACT Mastery* program averages more than a three point improvement in only six weeks, four times better than the national test prep average.

Contact Craig by email, on his blog, or on Facebook.

craig@actmastery.org
www.actmastery.org
http://www.facebook.com/CraigGehringACT

Further Study

For more information, and to find a prep course in your area or online, visit

WWW.ACTMASTERY.ORG

Classroom discounts available upon request.

Other Craig Gehring Titles:

SAT ACT Mastery
ACT Writing Mastery, Level 1
ACT Math Mastery, Level 1
ACT Reading Mastery, Level 1
ACT Science Mastery, Level 1
Math Elements